Other books by Author

WW I   The Battle Of The MInd

WW II   This My Cell

WW III   Scars And Memories

WW IV   Voices

WW V   Alone I Roam

WW VI   2020 Deepend

WW VII   Seven

WW VIII   My Mental State

... more will be revealed soon...

WAR WITHIN

WW VII:
SEVEN

VOLUME 7 OF 7

MICHAEL R. BANE

WESTBOW
PRESS®
A DIVISION OF THOMAS NELSON
& ZONDERVAN

WestBow Press books may be ordered through booksellers or by contacting:

WestBow Press
A Division of Thomas Nelson & Zondervan
1663 Liberty Drive
Bloomington, IN 47403
www.westbowpress.com
844-714-3454

Scripture taken from the King James Version of the Bible.

ISBN: 978-1-6642-3726-1 (sc)
ISBN: 978-1-6642-3727-8 (e)

Print information available on the last page.

WestBow Press rev. date: 06/22/2021

CONTENTS

Chapter 1 Welcome Home

Chapter 2 Without You

Chapter 3 Frayed

Chapter 4   Deeper

Chapter 5   Where You Are

Chapter 6   Issues

Chapter 7 Broken Wings

DEDICATION

I dedicate; Seven: WWVII to my grandchildren Eric, Joshua, Isabel. I love you three so much. I am so glad for the times we have spent together, and the many more to come. You have all motivated me to continue, and complete this series. "War Within". You may not even realize, but you have. Please take the best parts of me, and incorporate them into your lives. I learned a whole new level of love from each of you. Love yourself, be true to those you love, and always remember. God is there. He will never leave you, nor forsake you.

INTRO? WWVII

I knew for many years that I wanted to complete a series of books containing my poetry, and as I complete and arrange these poems. I realize, I want to keep writing. So there is a great chance, I will do more. I honestly hope the right person finds the right poem, and it reaches their spirit, and helps them in some kind of way. I am nothing without God. Thank you Lord, for using someone like me to do your work.

CHAPTER 1

WELCOME HOME

Luke 15:24a

For this my son was dead, and is alive again; he was lost, and is found.

KJV

WHEN IT WAS WRITTEN

THE PRODIGAL SON

Many days in my life I was tempted
Many lusts of the flesh I fell to these
Now I come back to you Father broken hearted
Now I come back to you Father on my knees

And He tells me welcome home son, your forgiven
And He tells me welcome home son, you are clean
And He tells me welcome home son, I still love you
Even more than the first day you believed

Now I come back to you Father
Now I come back to you Father
Now I come back broken hearted, on my knees

Many days in your life when you were tempted
Many lusts of the flesh, you fell to these
Now come back to your Father broken hearted
Now come back to your Father on your knees

And He'll tell you welcome home son, your forgiven
And He'll tell you welcome home son, you are clean
And He'll tell you welcome home son, I still love you
Even more than the first day you believed

So now come back to your Father
Come back to your Father
Come back broken hearted on your knees

Now we come back to you Father on our knees
We come back broken hearted, on our knees

BLESSED REDEMPTION

Blessed redemption
Forgiveness and love
It came from Jesus
It came through His blood

He is my savior
He is my Lord
When He went to calvary
And was nailed to that board

Blessed redemption
Now I am free
It came from Jesus
He did it for me

He is my savior
He is my Lord
Blessed redemption
For that I am sure

FORGIVENESS

Forgiveness, tell me what it means
It can mean so many things
Forgiveness from my thoughts, my deeds
to separate my wants, my needs
I forgive you, you forgive me
that is what it seems to be
It can mean so many things
to break the chains of hate, be free
to stop all the fighting, and start to agree
Forgiveness, share my hopes, my dreams
I can forgive you, because He forgave me
Forgiveness there's no end it seems
Forgiveness, tell me what it means
It can mean so many things
I must also learn to forgive me
For the things I did, for the things I've seen
that is what it seems to be
Forgiveness, there's no end it seems.

THROUGH THE BLOOD

Its through the blood
The precious blood of Jesus
Its through the blood
Spilled on Calgary.
Its through the blood
The precious blood of Jesus
Its through the blood
I'm chosen to believe.
Its through the blood
Its through the blood
Its through the blood
The precious blood of Jesus
Its through the blood
That I am finally free.
Its through the blood
Its through the blood

The precious blood of Jesus
Its through the blood
Every drop, for you, and me.
Its through the blood
The precious blood of Jesus
Its through the blood
Forgiveness, I receive.
Its through the blood
Its through the blood
Its through the blood
I'm chosen to believe.
Its through the blood
Poured out on that tree.
Its through the blood.
Forgiveness, I receive.
Its through the blood
That I am finally free.
Its through the blood
Its through the blood

MY GOD

I thank my God through words
I thank my God through deeds
I thank my God
by helping others with their needs
I thank my God
For the breath of life that He has given me
I thank my God
For creating you
a special, separate gift
only you can be you.
Created to help, to love
to worship only Him
You are His daughter
You are His son
I see my God through life
every things that has breath
My God breathes life, not death

I see my God through nature
the breeze through the high grasses
the bright colored flowers
the birds singing merrily
as they fly by.
The fish in the water
The stars in the sky.
I see my God through others
through little children,
Fathers, and mothers.
But most of all
through you
a special, separate gift.

HE REIGNS

Something I learned as I look
through the days
seeking pleasure
always causes pain
A moment of unselfishness
brings happiness, it rains
And the power of God
Flows through me
He Reigns -
Time cannot stand still
Those days turn to years
To deny myself
And think more of you
After all this is what
His word says to do
It's awesome to think
How simple it is
And we give God the glory
After all, it's All His ...

UNDER ONE GOD

I'm not a mistake
unmistakable
I'm not afraid
unshakable
I'm not a victim
untakable
I'm not a criminal
unfathomable
I'm not a animal
untamable
I'm not a crack
unbreakable
I'm not ashamed
under One God

CHAPTER 2

WITHOUT YOU

Joshua 1:5 c,d

I will be with thee; I will not fail thee,
nor forsake thee.

KJV

WHEN IT WAS WRITTEN

CLING TO LIFE

Fight your fight
Show your strength
Cling to life ...
No one there
but you.
No one knows
its true
Eternity at last
take his hand
No one knows
it true
No one there
but you.
To see you
Fight your fight
as you cling to life ...
but you.

DEJA VU

I can feel your love
its emotional
It's in the way you talk
it's just what you do
or is it Deja Vu?

They say loves
What you make it
And each day I give
a little bit more

I can feel your love
its devotional
So are you real
or just Deja Vu?

They say love is real
and each day I want
a little bit more

It's just what you do
or is it just Deja Vu?

YOUR LIST

Am I just on your list?

Does my name roll off your tongue
and through your lips?

Do you want my touch?

Do you need my kiss?

Or Am I just another on your list?

I LET HER GO

It's too late now for me
I let her go, you see.
In love together
But it's too late
I let her go.
I can not forget her
She doesn't remember me
I let her go.
And now it's too late

LOST WITHOUT YOU

I'm lost without you ...
I'm crushed without you ...
Watching you go, is so hard
Now I sit here without you ...
I wish I could make it right
What I did wrong
But it's too late
And it's so hard
Being here, without you ...
I wish I could fix
What I broken
And, I'm crushed without you
I need you to see
I'm lost without you ...

SO MANY SCARS

Who do you think you are?
going through life leaving scars
on everyone you meet

What gives you the right?
to hurt so many souls
to break so many hearts
and leave so many scars

It hurts in so many ways
What gives you the right?
And who do you think you are?

PIECE BY PIECE

Piece by piece
you take all of me
and there is nothing left to give.
you tore me apart piece by piece
Now what do I do?
I don't have the pieces
to put myself back together again.
you tore me apart piece by piece
Can you please come back?
and help to put me back together again
piece by piece.
Because there's nothing here left of me.
You took all of me
When you left me here with me
piece by piece.

FOR YOUR HEAD

I wake up, I see you there
So I smile and sneak out of bed

As I tiptoe across the room
to make some coffee for your head ...

Life is good
And it's better with you

Theirs endless possibilities
So much I wanna do.

So much I wanna tell you
so much I wanna say

But if I told you everything
I'm afraid you wouldn't stay.

So for now, I'll just stay quiet
and, make some coffee for your head ...

CHAPTER 3

FRAYED

Proverbs 14:32

The wicked is driven away in his wickedness:
but the righteous hath hope in his death.

KJV

WHEN IT WAS WRITTEN

MONSTER ME

Inside my mind
Monster me
So many things
You cannot see
   you look...
    you listen...
So many things
You can not hear
Inside my mind
Monster me
though I am
a new creature
He still lives
Inside my mind
Monster me
Do not awaken him
He is asleep
Let him rest
It is for all the best
To keep him
inside my mind
Monster me

THE REAL ME

Will I let you see the real me?...
Take off my masks
and just believe?
My heart is full
it's full of dreams
The depth from where
I came it seems
that maybe, just maybe
you will understand
Maybe you will help
If I let you see the real me ...
    and open my heart
    share my dreams
Will you help?
If I take off my masks
and show you the real me ...

WHERE IS MY SOUL?

A heart of black
a twisted mind
body not mine
All of this
Where is my sou
Life is over
Now, where do I go?
My spirit lives
too late to change
dust, returns to earth
Where is my soul?
Nothing else matters
Now, where will I go?

DARKNESS

The war within
The battle of the mind
The choices that surface
They start deep inside

Do I choose to remember?
Do I choose to forget?
Why do I continue?
Is this really worth the fight?

Darkness chokes me
It's hard to breathe
Darkness surrounds me
It's hard to see

Darkness inside me
The war within
The light in the tunnel
Is growing dim

I can't go on
My life, my sin
The battle is over
Darkness, you win

?

Is this a thought ?
A vision ?
Is this reality ?
Ideas, words ?
Thought into existence?
Dreaming out loud ?
Sleep will not come ?
Did you see that ?
Silence, deadly ?
Shapes, colors ?
Things to come ?
Things past ?
Not now, when ?
What was that ?
Tasting the colors ?
Seeing the particles, air ?
Creepy, brings a chill ?
But I'm not afraid ?
What does it all mean ?
Does it matter ?
What is matter ?
Good-bye for now ?
Sleep will not come ?

I AM AFRAID

My heart is frayed
I am afraid
The games I played
choices I made
I must repay
all that I took away
I am afraid
My heart it frayed
I need you Jesus
I believe
Forgive me Lord
These days, these nights
They all connect
This time I take
Time to reflect
I am afraid
My heart is frayed
Forgive me Lord
My heart is frayed
I am afraid

WAR CHILD

Search and destroy
War child, open your eyes
Someone better save my soul
Help me change my mind
Before it's too late
Forgotten, but not dead
Search, and destroy
This is happening, this is real
Open your eyes, war child
dance with destruction
the final intrusion
Now, it's too late
One string of life, snapped
War child
Forgotten, but not dead
blurred vision
thoughts obscured
Not even a word
one squeeze, last breath
death wins
this is real...

MORE LIKE YOU

Can I help you
not to hurt anymore?
And to help you smile
like you did before?

Can I help you
to wipe your tears?
And erase your pain
bottled up through the years?

Can I help you
to become more like you?
And less like them?
Can I help you?

CHAPTER 4

DEEPER

Isaiah 41:10a, b

Fear thou not; For I am with thee; be not dismayed; For I am thy God.

KJV

WHEN IT WAS WRITTEN

TEACH ME, LORD

Teach me, Lord to pray
Show me the way -
I know I talk to you ...
in my own way -
though, I want to go deeper
Take me, Lord to the next level
Lord, I honor you ...
of you, I am at awe
So many distractions
And outside stimuli
I can not quiet the noise inside
even silence has a sound -
All I have is Yours
Everything I am is because of you ...
Teach me, Lord to listen
Take me to that place
My heart, mind, and spirit
All, now one because of you ...
If you can do that
    you, can do this -
Teach me, Lord to pray
Teach me, Lord to listen
Take me, to that place

PAID IN FULL

We are children of the day
We live in the light
We are not in the darkness
We are not of the night

Love, and comfort in our hearts
Knit together, we can not come apart
Honest lips, they please the Lord
The free gift He gave
We can never afford

The price was paid
    Paid in full
Let's praise His name
He broke the chain

Our mouths must speak
Our tongues, a flame
We can not sleep, we must awake

When He returns
Its us, He'll take

ALL GOOD THINGS

All good things ...
are there for you

You can have
all good things ...

All good things ...
come to those

You deserve
all good things ...

All good things ...
are not good for <u>you</u>

IN GODS HANDS

One day at a time
Its only one day
That's all that we get
That's all that I need
Yesterday is gone, and
Tomorrow is not here
Neither is it promised
So, I'll live for today
Of course I have goals
Of course I'll make plans
But, if I get tomorrow
Well, that's in God's hands ...

THE BEATEN PATH

As I walk down the beaten path
Prairie all around
Pretty yellow flowers abound
   the sky so big
   the white puffy cloud
A broken fence allows me to pass
In the distance, a mountain found
so many colors
blue, green, purple, brown
I hear a trickling brook
the trout jumps for a fly
has his breakfast
with a splash
I sit to rest
I look at everything
Speechless, I can not talk
A tear rolls down my cheek
I lay back, close my eyes
Falling asleep, I dream
My dreams cannot compare
to what I saw today
As I walked down the beaten path

I SURRENDER ALL

I don't have to be afraid
I am surrounded by angels
To my left, to my right
When I surrender, and no longer fight
My angels lead me, guide me
To do what's right
When I stay on the path
I don't have to be afraid
I am surrounded
Surrounded by angels
When I stay on the path
And no longer fight
I surrender all -
And I live in victory
I am surrounded by angels
And have peace
And it comes when,
I surrender all -

LOVE SOMEONE

Why are you so sad?
don't be afraid to cry
Why are you alone?
don't be afraid to try

To love someone
And let someone love you

So don't close your eyes
to what's going on outside
don't close yourself in

Don't be sad
And don't be afraid

To love someone
And let someone love you

DON'T YOU DARE QUIT

Don't run from your pain
Write about it
Let it become your inspiration
and don't you dare quit ...

Don't run from your fear
Face it
Let it become your strength
and don't you dare quit...

Don't run from your God
Run to Him
Let Him become your all
and don't you dare quit...
    EVER

CHAPTER 5

WHERE YOU ARE

Revelation 3:8b

Behold, I have set before thee an open door, and no man can shut it.

KJV

WHEN IT WAS WRITTEN

THE DOOR

I am the one who holds the key to my heart
their is only one way in
I must open the door, and let you in
You cannot push, shove, or force your way
You cannot trick, or manipulate.

I allow no drama, or chaos take residence
you see, I have choices today
I choose who I allow in
I decide if you are positive, or destructive

If the door remains closed
you cannot come in

If I open the door and let you in
you are welcome

I will share everything I have
My goals, my dreams, my hope, my love
I will also share my sorrows, my pains

And if you choose to open the door to me
and allow me in
I will share everything you have
Your goals, your dreams, your hope, your love
I will also share your sorrows, your pains

You are the only one who holds the key to your heart
their is only one way in
You must open the door, and let me in.

MIRACLE WORLD

I'm living in a miracle world -
From where I've come
to see you now
there is no explanation
so don't even try to justify
look at your life
the truth, the lies
Why are you here?
where you are now
the depths and the distance
no coincidence
that we share this space, this time
I'm living in a miracle world -
I am no longer dead
I joined the living
I looked at my life
the truth, the lies
there is no explanation
All is all, and none is none
The depths from where I've come
Nothing short of a miracle
Can't begin to explain
This is why I know
I'm living in a miracle world -

GET YOU ALONE

I always got by on my own
Till I met you
Now it tears me to the bone
I love you, and how
Will I get you alone?

It seems that we were
torn from the same cloth
It can't be destroyed by
fire, or moth

I love you, and how
will I get you alone?

THE GATE

The gate is locked
and the lock is rusty, and jammed
Because nobody dares to enter
and nobody cared enough to try

Maybe, I can open it
Maybe, my key will fit
with a little work, and patience
elbow grease, and grit

The lock may fall, and the gate may open
who knows what blessings await
I see a trail but it
always stops at the gate.

I choose, I dare enter
life is not always better on the other side
But, I must see for myself

It can't stop at the gate
There has to be more
And, I care enough to try

Maybe, my key will fit
Maybe I can open it
Maybe I can enter

And maybe my life will change
on the other side of the gate.

NO ONE GOES

Oh what you do to me
no one knows

So would you go with me
where no one goes?

What would you
do to me

If we went where
no one goes?

And would you make sure
that no one knows

If I took you with me
where no one goes?

TWO DOORS

One door closes
and another one is opened
Both by my Lord -
Now the choice is mine ...
Do I stand at the closed door?
afraid, worried, confused
trying a key that does not fit,
or to kick it in?
Or do I walk through
the opened door?
opened by my Lord -
with hope, confidence, and peace
Now the choice is mine ...
Two doors - one past, one now
the two doors may look the same
but, oh - they are so different
Now the choice is mine ...
I choose the open door
the door opened by my Lord -

CHAPTER 6

ISSUES

Ecclesiastes 3:17

I said in mine heart, God shall judge the righteous and the wicked;
for there is a time for every purpose and for every work.

KJV

WHEN IT WAS WRITTEN

I -   Hole, 2010

II -   Issues, 2020

III -   Out of Control, 2020

IV -   King of the Raff, 2020

V -   Over It, 2020

VI -   System Down, 2020

VII -   Anxious Moments, 2021

HOLE

That deep, empty hole
They call it your spirit
They call it your soul
Darkness so thick
The darkness so full
So is it too late?
to change your mind?
to change your fate?
to fill the hole
Awaken your spirit
escape from the sickness
add light, new existence
They call it your soul
it always was
and will always be
you know what is real
that darkness so full
darkness so thick
you still have breath
it's not too late
you need the light
to fill your soul
a spiritual cleansing of
that deep empty hole ...

ISSUES

You have your issues
and I have mine to

I have so many
but, you just a few

Could you please accept me
like I accepted you?

Issues, are not who we are
but, just the things we do

And though I have so many
And though you have a few

Would you please accept me
like I accepted you?

Maybe you can help me
and I can help you to

Issues: huh
Now, what do we do?

OUT OF CONTROL

What have I become?
What have I done?

From last to first
From best to worst

I search my heart
I search my soul

I'm out of my mind
I'm out of control

Is it from without?
Is it from within?

A dark, could heart
A cold, dark soul

Out of my mind
Out of control

What have I done?
What have I become?

KING OF THE RAFF

You are too good a girl
and, I am too bad a man

So if you decide to love me
just know where I stand

You came from the suburbs
Me, the wrong side of the tracks

So if you decide to love me
can you see me, not my past?

You are too good of a girl
and, I am the king of the raff

But if you decide to love me
I will give my all to make it last

So kiss me once, but please understand
I've been around this insane land

Give me your heart
and, I'll give you my hand

And if you decide to love me
I'll love you back

I promise to give my all
to make it last

Just remember what I've told you
just remember where I stand

You are too good a girl
And, I am too bad a man ...

OVER IT

Why you judge so hard?
Why you such a hypocrite?

Be careful what you ask for
you might just get it

    And you reap
    From which you sow

So watch how you judge
What gives you the right?

Practice what you preach
You are such a hypocrite

    And, I'm under and
    over it ...

SYSTEM DOWN

System down, I need some power
my heart is black, and
my soul is sour

It feels like this might be
the twelfth hour

The bell tolls internal
time is not time
Now time is eternal

The tables are turned
Full reversal

System down
we have a problem
with no solution

My heart is black
my soul is sour

- Internal desolution -

ANXIOUS MOMENTS

My anxiety
creeps inside of me
makes it hard to see
is this really me?
My thoughts are deceived
its harder to breathe
heat takes over me
whys this have to be?
my anxiety

CHAPTER 7

BROKEN WINGS

Psalms 91:11

For He shall give His angels charge over thee, to keep thee in all thy ways.

KJV

WHEN IT WAS WRITTEN

NEVER ALONE

I'm surrounded by angels
I'm never alone.
As I take this walk down this
long winding road.
And, I feel I can't take another step
And they lift me, and carry me
So I can rest.
They give me hope, they give me strength
But most of all, I'm never alone.
So I must stay on the narrow road.
Because that is where my angels are.
They remind me, I'm never alone
When I come to another fork in the road
To make a choice, to the left or the right
To know if I need to flee, or to fight
Just to know that I am never alone
Along this journey
Along this road
I'm surrounded by angels
I'm never alone.

THE LAND OF THE LIVING

When I choose to live
death loses its grip on me
I turn my back on death
and join the land of the living

And, now I see life
My heart lives, and loves
It's because of you
You showed me the way
to the land of the living

And each day I live
And each day I love
It's because of you
But I must choose to live
And stay in the land of the living

I was dead
But now I live
And it's because of you
That I am here in the land of the living

YOU CAN FLY

Don't close your eyes
Don't close your eyes
Keep them open, look at life
Use your vision, don't be blind
To what is going on outside
life is there for you to find
Don't close your eyes
Don't close your eyes
Learn to mingle, don't be shy
like an eagle you can fly
you can soar
higher, higher than before
Dry your eyes, don't you cry
You are free, free to fly
Set some goals, set them high
there is no limit, but the sky
Don't close your eyes
Don't close your eyes
Keep them open, live your life

PEACE I SEEK

To search for love
Its peace I seek
Quick to listen
Slow to speak
Open to learn
Willing to teach
Courage to change
Set goals to reach
Wisdom to know
To be quiet, and meek
To search for love
Its peace I seek
To know what I sow
That I will reap
With God in my life
It's Him that I seek
To search for love
Its peace I seek

MY ANGELS

My angels hands are never idle
they hold blessings
They close around prayers, and thoughts
my love of angels is never idle
It grows with each thought, and blessing
as my interest grows
and my faith grows
The study of my angels begins
The story of my angels will never cease
My angels hearts, and spirits
are open to me, and connect with mine
In turn, they connect me to God
My angels wings surround me
I am never alone
God sent my angels to bring me home
To guide me until that time
My angels know my time
They also connect me to you
and your angels
Their speed, their power, their love
My angels ...

DISCONNECTED

The invisible cord
from the heart to the head

Mine is disconnected
my feelings are dead

How did things end up
this way?

By the way I lived
by the choices I made

Sometimes I don't care
that's just the fact

Thankfully my spirits
in tact

My cords disconnected
I can not feel

So watch yours close
This is real ...

WITHOUT WINGS

As impossible as it
   seems
I'm flying without wings
I think about
   so many things
And so much joy
   to me, you bring
And as insane as it
   seems
Because of you
I'm flying without wings

OUT ALIVE

Barely made it out alive
but I'm alright
So when you look in my eyes
it may make it easier to realize
Everytime the demons rise
My angel grabs his sword, he flies
The battle is not up in the skies
The war is with me, inside
So when its time to flee, or fight
I won't be alone
I will make it out alive
And, I'm alright ...

Printed in the United States
by Baker & Taylor Publisher Services